TANA HOBAN

I Read Signs

Greenwillow
Books
New York

This one
is for
all my
children

With many thanks
to all the sign-finders

I Read Signs
Copyright © 1983 by Tana Hoban
All rights reserved.
Manufactured in China.
For information address
HarperCollins Children's
Books, a division of
HarperCollins Publishers,
10 East 53rd Street,
New York, NY 10022.
www.harperchildrens.com
First Edition
11 12 13 SCP
20 19 18 17 16
Library of Congress
Cataloging in Publication Data

Hoban, Tana.
I read signs.
"Greenwillow Books."
Summary: Introduces signs
and symbols frequently
seen along the street.
1. Traffic signs and signals
—Juvenile literature.
2. Street signs—
Juvenile literature.
3. Signs and signboards—
Juvenile literature.
[1. Traffic signs and signals.
2. Street signs.
3. Signs and signboards.
4. Signs and symbols]
I. Title.
TE228.H63 1983
001.55'2   83-1482
ISBN 0-688-02317-7 (trade)
ISBN 0-688-02318-5 (lib. bdg.)
ISBN 0-688-07331-X (pbk.)

NO LEFT
TURN

NO STANDING

EXPRESS

DEPT OF TRANSPORTATION

DEAD
END

TOWN OF BRIGHTON